New Mags City Guide
London

For years, I've traveled the world as a design and lifestyle expert. Every time I discover an inspiring place, I make a note of it. Over time, this list has grown to include many outstanding destinations. People often ask me for travel recommendations. Obviously, most people don't have the time to find the best spots, because it requires time, and time is a scarce resource for many. That's why we created this series of city guides. Not just any collection of guides, but the best, most beautiful, and most practical, presented as a real book. I believe the ideal city guide is tangible, something you can bring along on your journey, especially handy when your smartphone runs out of battery.

Special thanks to Jesper Svangård from New Mags for his enthusiasm and publishing expertise, and to Mario Depicolzuane, our art director, whose studio's design brought this guide to life. I'm also deeply grateful to all the incredible locations featured and to everyone who helped bring this project to life.

We hope that you, as a reader, will embrace our city guide and find it valuable on your travels. After all, that's the true purpose of this book.

CONTINENTAL
SANDWICH
BAR
ENDS

TABLE OF CONTENTS

UNDERGROUND
COVENT

London is cool, not in a sharp, posh kind of way. It's the kind of coolness that comes from within. A quiet confidence, born of centuries of history and constant reinvention. One day it's grey and rain-soaked, the next it's neon-lit and electric. The city wears its melancholy like a trench coat, always a little damp at the seams, yet impeccably dressed.

Nothing here is just one thing. It's gritty and polished at the same time. Think Soho at night: a neon-lit maze of bars and clubs. Or Shoreditch, with its quirky cafés and galleries where edgy art and vintage jackets hang side by side.

Swinging London, somehow it still lingers in the air like an echo from the 60s, when Mods on scooters filled the streets and The Rolling Stones shook the world. But this city isn't nostalgic. It keeps reinventing itself. From punk and new wave to dandy and boho, from royal pageantry to underground rebellion, London has always made space for both palaces and political protest.

Whether you're here for Savile Row suits, tea-soaked rituals in Notting Hill or second-hand shopping in Shoreditch, it's hard not to fall a little bit in love with London's imperfect perfection.

BENS
of Primrose Hill
BENS
MEAN GIRLS
BENS
MOUNEYRAC

174
PIES

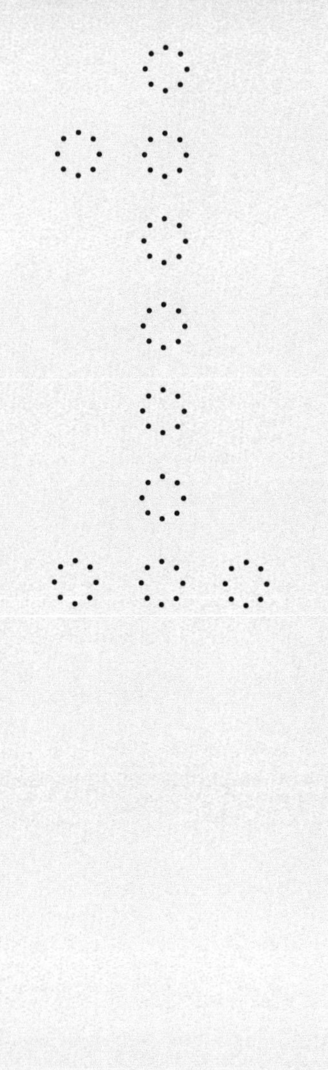

Art'otel London Battersea Power Station
Bermonds Locke
Inhabit Southwick Street
Lime Tree Hotel
One Hundred Shoreditch
Shoreditch House
The Hoxton Southwark
The Lost Poet
The Newman

Stay

The Monocle Guide To Better Living
Row
POSTMODERN ARCHITECTURE
LESS IS A BORE

Art'otel London Battersea Power Station

1 Electric Blvd, Nine Elms
London SW11 8BJ

@artotel
artotellondonbattersea.com
+44 333 400 6152

Set within the striking Foster + Partners-designed Battersea Roof Gardens, this 164-room hotel is part of the new Electric Boulevard, a sleek mix of homes, offices and a pedestrian high street just south of the iconic Power Station. Interiors have been designed by art'otel's award-winning signature artist Jaime Hayon, whose bold, colourful and playful aesthetic style is alive in every corner. The hotel's artistic concept features original art displayed from Hayon, with interiors inspired by the Power Station's history and heritage. Being the first UK opening for the art'otel brand, the launch brings a bold new energy to the ground-breaking Battersea Power Station neighbourhood.

In the shadow of Pink Floyd's iconic power station, Art'otel Battersea Power Station is part of the 1930s landmark's bold new chapter.

Bermonds Locke

157 Tower Bridge Road
London SE1 3LW

@lockehotels
lockeliving.com
+44 207 052 7170

Just across the iconic Tower Bridge and the old Shad Thames, you'll find yourself in the bustling heart of Bermondsey. Bermonds Locke opened in 2020 as the third London outpost from lifestyle hospitality brand Locke. It's a home-meets-hotel concept with 143 apartments, each featuring fully fitted kitchens, laundry facilities, and generous living space.

Bermonds Locke also houses a destination restaurant, co-working areas, a bar, and a workout studio.

The creative vision and interiors come courtesy of London-based studio Holloway Li. Paying tribute to the beauty of nature, both aesthetically and in terms of sustainability, they've crafted a distinctive living experience using repurposed construction materials throughout the public areas and private apartments.

Locke's signature studios bring the shifting gradient of a desert sunset to South London. Upper floors are awash in soft blues, beiges, and greys, while lower levels are drenched in saturated pinks. The concept was developed in collaboration with Heather Tierney of Wanderlust, the visionary behind cult US restaurant The Butcher's Daughter.

Bermonds Locke channels the laid-back spirit of Southern California, think Joshua Tree, the Mojave Desert, and Abbot Kinney, reimagined in a corner of London that's fast becoming a destination in its own right.

Think Joshua Tree meets Tower Bridge. Bermonds Locke brings a sun-washed slice of SoCal cool to the heart of Bermondsey.

Alvar Aalto
LONDON
ELEMENTAL LIVING

Inhabit Southwick Street

25–27 Southwick St, Paddington
London W2 1JQ

@inhabit_hotels
southwick.inhabithotels.com
+44 207 479 2333

If tranquillity, Georgian townhouses steeped in history, and timeless Scandinavian design speak to your soul, then Inhabit Southwick Street is the place to check in. Tucked away in Paddington, this calming oasis is spread across six beautifully restored Georgian homes.

Visually, it draws inspiration from a bygone era, but the concept feels firmly rooted in the now, a modern take on luxury that centres on peace, quality, wellness, and a strong stance on sustainability. And it all fits seamlessly into Paddington's quietly understated vibe.

The look is slightly eclectic: a blend of classic British details, mid-century Nordic design, and laid-back Californian lifestyle. The hotel's wellness offerings include a well-equipped gym, an infrared sauna, a meditation pod, and daily yoga and pilates sessions.

Inhabit's plant-based restaurant, Yeotown, extends the wellness philosophy to the plate, serving up seasonal, nourishing food. Breakfast highlights include Blueberry Butterfly Pancakes and "Yeotown Style" Eggs Benedict, followed by hearty lunch and dinner dishes like colourful bowls, curries, and vegan burgers. Drinks are just as thoughtful, conscious cocktails, mindful mocktails, cold-pressed juices, smoothies, and adaptogenic lattes.

Paddington's got that just-right mix of café chatter, leafy strolls, and canal charm.

MIES VAN DER ROHE
TASCHEN
Bradbury Thompson
The Art of Graphic Design
Yale

Lime Tree Hotel

135–137 Ebury Street
London SW1W 9QU

@limetreehotel
limetreehotel.co.uk
+44 207 730 8191

Lime Tree Hotel spans two historic townhouses at the corner of Ebury Street and Elizabeth Street, often dubbed "London's prettiest street." The postcode is quintessential Belgravia, and it might all sound a bit grand, but the atmosphere is anything but. Instead, it's a quiet, unpretentious haven tucked into the heart of fast-paced London.

Set in a beautifully preserved 19th-century Grade II-listed building, the hotel is full of original character. Many of the rooms feature classic townhouse details: high ceilings, open fireplaces, and ornate cornicing. Some come with French doors and small balconies overlooking the street, while others are more compact, ideal for solo travellers, with views of the leafy walled garden.

You're in London, practically neighbours with Buckingham Palace (aka Britain's biggest council house, if you ask a cabbie), so go on, treat yourself to an afternoon tea, a cocktail, or both. The Buttery's got just the right amount of charm for a royal-worthy pause.

Two Georgian townhouses stitched together with good coffee, creaky floors, and Belgravia charm.

One Hundred Shoreditch

100 Shoreditch High Street
London E1 6JQ

@onehundredshoreditch
onehundredshoreditch.com
+44 207 613 9800

One Hundred Shoreditch is the blueprint for the quintessential Gen Z–approved East London design hotel. On weekdays, the lobby buzzes with freelancers armed with MacBooks, scattered across sofas and communal worktables. Shoreditch, and East London more broadly, was reinvented in the '90s by the hipster generation. While many of the original artists have since moved further east, a new wave of creatives has claimed the neighbourhood in the roaring twenties. It's a little less gritty these days, but the cool factor remains firmly intact.

Even the address tells a story. One Hundred Shoreditch was born from the bones of the iconic Ace Hotel, East London's hipster hangout that defined the creative scene in the millennial decade. Its successor brings a more grown-up, polished energy to the neighbourhood, without losing the area's signature edge.

The interiors of One Hundred Shoreditch were designed by Jacu Strauss, Creative Director at Lore Group. Strauss reimagined the former Ace Hotel space with a muted palette of sheepskin, leather, jute, and raffia, materials that bring warmth and texture. The result, especially on the upper floors, is a calming retreat that offers a more mature, laid-back take on East London cool. Jan Hendzel Studio contributed a series of benches and sculptural pieces crafted from reclaimed and green timber, adding a tactile, sustainable layer to the hotel's public spaces.

Same address, new vibe, the Ace spirit lives on, trading sneakers for loafers.

Shoreditch House

1 Ebor Street
London E1 6AW

@sohohouse
sohohouse.com
+44 207 739 5040

High above the bustle, in the old Tea Building, Shoreditch House, part of Soho House, is basically East London's ultimate glow-up spot. By day, it's laptops and flat whites in the library, or a quick workout at the gym downstairs. By night, the lights dim, the cocktails flow, and the heated rooftop pool becomes the place to be.

Inside, it's all vintage, warehouse coolness meeting cosy club vibe: exposed brick, huge windows framing the skyline, squishy Chesterfields, and pops of cherry-red that look made for your Instagram grid. There's a wellness crew on hand if you're into spa days, but honestly, the vibe is more "work hard, play harder", with just enough time for a rooftop swim in between teams meetings. Whether it's the view, the vibe, or the striped sunloungers, Shoreditch House bursts with East London energy, turned all the way up.

Part of the Soho House creative family, Shoreditch House mixes dining, workspaces, and a calendar of members-only events.

The Hoxton Southwark

32–40 Blackfriars Road
London SE1 8NY

@thehoxtonhotel
thehoxton.com
+44 207 903 3000

South of the Thames, located between Tate Modern and Borough Market, you'll find one of London's most dialled-in Gen Z hotels, arguably the only one of its kind this side of the river.

The Hoxton Southwark is built for and fuelled by creative energy: the lobby buzzes with freelancers and micro-entrepreneurs armed with Macbook Pros, notebooks and designer tote bags. The superfast Wi-Fi flows freely from the taps, right alongside freshly brewed coffee and craft beer, and the bar stays open well into the night. In other words, there's absolutely no excuse not to work late.

The interior aesthetic strikes a balance between exposed brick walls, lush greenery, and art-covered surfaces. Downstairs, the restaurant Albie mixes marble tabletops with Art Deco lamps and pastel velvet chairs, like a soft-spoken New York reference dropped into the middle of Southwark. Upstairs, the rooms continue the story with high wood-panelled headboards, marble accents, and local artwork by emerging talents. There are five room categories, Shoebox, Snug, Cosy, Roomy, and Biggy, offering options for every taste, space need, and budget.

Once an industrial powerhouse, Southwark still hums with creative energy, from warehouse galleries to world-class markets.

The Lost Poet

6 Portobello Road
London W11 3DG

@thelostpoetportobello
thelostpoet.co.uk
+44 207 243 6604

Creating a boutique hotel on one of London's most iconic streets, Portobello Road, in picture-perfect Notting Hill, sets the bar high. And yet, The Lost Poet, a four-room townhouse hotel, delivers beautifully, embracing the philosophy that small really is beautiful.

The design concept comes from Cubic Studios, a local property design team born and bred in Notting Hill. The townhouse feels like a poetic love letter to the neighbourhood, celebrating its creativity and charm through four individually designed bedrooms. Each space, The Suite, The Quarters, The Salon, and The Muse, has its own distinct mood, style, and colour story. Think modern art, reclaimed wood panelling, marble bathrooms with British brassware, and bold, personality-filled wallpaper. This place is basically a masterclass in Brit-cool collabs, think mood-setting scents by Lola James Harper, bold tiles from House of Hackney, Maison C wallpaper with serious attitude, and wild textiles from Timorous Beasties. It's modern with a nostalgic twist, romantic with an edge, and it totally works.

The Newman

50 Newman Street
London W1T 3EB

@thenewmanlondon
thenewman.com

Tucked into its namesake Newman Street, The Newman is the debut hotel from Kinsfolk & Co, a new international hospitality brand making its mark in London. Perfectly placed in Fitzrovia, where Bloomsbury's literary spirit meets Soho's sartorial flair, the hotel blends right into the neighbourhood's creative rhythm.

London-based studio Lind + Almond is behind the interiors, crafting a design language that bridges eras and personalities. Their vision is quietly opulent: Victorian influences mingle with Art Deco gestures, expressed through rich timber panelling, deep olive and burnt red tones, and stainless-steel details that add a contemporary edge. The aesthetic channels Fitzrovia's golden years, paying homage to its bohemian icons, most notably, the ever-defiant Nancy Cunard.

The hotel features 81 rooms and suites, all echoing the same layered elegance. The signature rooftop suite includes a private terrace and can be configured into a grand four-bedroom apartment. Downstairs, the street-level brasserie and cocktail bar are social by design, while the spa below celebrates Nordic simplicity with minimal, functional spaces built for both indulgence and restoration.

In literary Fitzrovia, once the haunt of Dylan Thomas and Virginia Woolf, The Newman now writes its own boutique chapter.

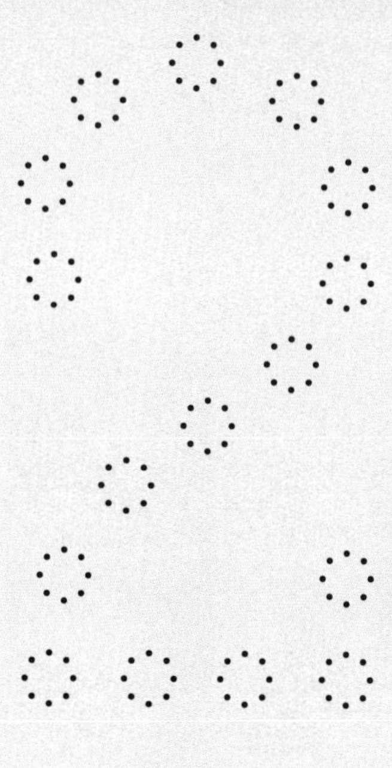

Jolene Bakery & Restaurant
Common Breads
Kuro Coffee
Café Cecilia
Café Petiole
The River Café Café
Perilla
Greenberry Café
Goodbye Horses
Brawn
Toklas
St. JOHN Bread and Wine
St. JOHN Smithfield
Rochelle Canteen
Leo's Bar and Restaurant
Morchella
Oma
Noisy Oyster
Sessions Arts Club
Cadet
Bar Italia
Sager + Wilde

Taste

JOLENE

Jolene Bakery and Restaurant

21 Newington Green
Stoke Newington
London N16 9PU

@jolene_newingtongreen
jolenebakery.com
+44 203 887 2309

There's a small, green oasis in North London, just south of Stoke Newington, between Highbury and Dalston. In and around this green pocket known as Newington Green, those in the know have quietly begun to gather. What makes the area special is that it hasn't (yet) been hit by the full wave of gentrification that pushed the creative scene from Shoreditch to London Fields and now sees Newington Green as the next frontier.

Everything here is described as "leafy," and for good reason. It's also here, in leafy Newington Green, that you'll find the "original" Jolene, a bakery and restaurant overlooking the square. Jolene opened in 2018, so it's hardly a hidden gem, but still under the radar for many visitors. The coffee is excellent, and their freshly baked bread and pastries are worth the journey alone. Pastries, pasta and pizza are all made in-house.

The concept has been so successful, it's since spawned three more Jolene bakeries and two restaurants, Primeur and Western Laundry, all located in the northeastern quadrant of the city.

Common Breads

110 Buckingham Palace Road
London SW1W 9SA

@commonbreads
commonbreads.com
+44 208 017 3773

Lebanese street food reimagined as an architectural daydream. The place opened in May 2024 in London's Belgravia, founded by childhood friends Abbas Fawaz, Abbas Zein and Kamal El Zein. Less a restaurant, more a modern-day bakehouse with serious Lebanese soul.

Designed by local firm MA Studio, the interior balances warmth and precision: wood-panelled walls, archways, and shelves lined with cookbooks and pantry items, like za'atar and a variety of flavoured tahini are displayed for sale. Two L-shaped counters tiled in a black-and-white checkerboard pattern (a nod to Lebanon's love for backgammon) frame the open kitchen, where bakers shape dough with meditative focus. The industrial flooring subtly mimics sesame seeds, scattered across both the floor and much of the menu.

Look up and you'll see ka'ak-inspired light fixtures by Fabraca Studios; look around, and you'll spot images by Beirut-based photographer Tanya Traboulsi, offering a poetic glimpse into everyday baking rituals. When the sun's out, head to the 10-seat terrace for a coffee and something fresh from the oven.

Common Breads is a fresh take on Lebanese Street Food with a modern London twist.

MADE TO ORDER
KA'AK
MANOUCHE

The Royal Borough of Kensington and Chelsea
HILLGATE STREET. W.8.
KURO COFFEE
Unsuitable for HGVs

Kuro Coffee

3 Hillgate Street
London W8 7SP

@kuro_london
kuro-london.com

A favourite Notting Hill coffee spot, Kuro Coffee is where locals linger, perched on the bench outside if the sun's out, or tucked into the small, minimalist interior when London does its thing. It's got that East London vibe that somehow found its way west, mixing Japanese precision with a hint of South Korean café culture. The downstairs space hums with energy, all white walls and clean lines, while an extra floor upstairs offers a quieter escape if you're staying for a second cup. As the name hints, *Kuro* means black, a nod to the pure, fresh-brewed coffee that's the real star here. They're serious about their craft, from meticulous pour-overs to creamy mochas, and they don't slack on the baked goods either, thanks to their own Kuro Bakery just around the corner.

Café Cecilia

32 Andrews Road
London E8 4FX

@cafececilialondon
cafececilia.com
+44 203 478 6726

Since opening in 2021 along the Regent's Canal, Café Cecilia has quickly become a favourite among East London's design-conscious crowd. Helmed by chef Max Rocha, whose CV includes The River Café and St. John Bread & Wine, the café blends Irish heritage with contemporary European influences.

The interiors are minimal yet warm, echoing the simplicity of the menu, seasonal, unfussy, and beautifully executed. From boiled eggs with Guinness bread to pork chop with colcannon, each dish reflects a quiet confidence and deep-rooted culinary sensibility.

Named after Rocha's grandmother, Café Cecilia is personal without being sentimental. Whether you're stopping by for a late breakfast or settling in for dinner, it offers a sense of calm and clarity that's increasingly rare in the city.

Café Cecilia is named after chef Max Rocha's grandmother, proof that East London's coolest café also keeps it in the family.

vermouth & soda
white port & tonic
gin & tonic
vodka & tonic
vieille prune
calvados
pineau des charentes

CAFÉ PETIOLE

Café Petiole

South Wing, Somerset House, The Strand
London WC2R 1LA

@cafepetiole
cafepetiole.co.uk

Café Petiole is a plant-first café and restaurant tucked into the South Wing of Somerset House, one of London's most iconic settings. Named after the slender stalk that connects a plant's stem to its leaf, it's a nod to the kitchen's close connection to nature, both in philosophy and on the plate.

The menu is a vibrant spread of plant-focused small plates, fresh bakes, desserts, and salads, available to enjoy in the airy dining room or to take away for a stroll along the Thames. Inspiration comes from European travels, but the ingredients speak of the season, colourful, fresh, and handled with a light, confident touch.

With sweeping views of Somerset House's neoclassical courtyard, the café offers a serene backdrop for lingering over coffee or a leisurely lunch. The interiors nod to the idea of an artist's café, balancing historic elegance with a contemporary twist.

Named after the leaf's stalk, Café Petiole turns botany into brunch at Somerset House.

CAFÉ PETIOLE

The River Café Café

Thames Wharf, Rainville Road
London W6 9HA

@therivercafecafe
rivercafe.co.uk/river-cafe-cafe
+44 207 386 4200

Since 1987, The River Café has quietly held court on the Thames, not only redefining Italian food in London but serving as the launchpad for a whole generation of star chefs (yes, Jamie Oliver too). Back then, it was very much a product of its time: late-'80s indulgence in luxury, white tablecloths, fancy wines, and a taste for the rare and expensive. Eating at The River Café was a statement, not just a meal.

Fast forward to 2024: a new era, with shifting ideas of what quality and luxury mean. Perfect timing for a younger, looser sibling to arrive, The River Café Café, right next door. The interior swaps polished formality for breezy charm, a light-filled space with an easygoing energy its famous neighbour never had. The menu is pure River Café DNA, seasonal Italian favourites made from flawless ingredients, only here they come at friendlier prices.

Perilla

1–3 Green Lanes
Newington Green
London N16 9BS

@perilladining
perilladining.co.uk
+44 207 359 0779

Perilla is the epitome of Newington Green dining: earnest and low-key confident. Since opening in 2016, chef Ben Marks (former Claridge's, Noma, The Square) and restaurateur Matthew Emmerson (former Polpo and Polpetto) have made it the go-to for modern N16 diners who care as much about aesthetics as flavour. Plates arrive like little still lifes, small works of art perfectly arranged for pleasure and Instagram. It's anti–fine dining. Fancy food without the fine-dining price tag. The menu shifts with the seasons, offered as a finely tuned tasting journey or a more relaxed à la carte, while the wine list keeps pace, always sharp and surprising. The room itself mirrors the food. There are no white tablecloths. Instead, you'll experience raw, handcrafted materials, distressed surfaces, and floor-to-ceiling windows that frame leafy views of Newington Green.

Perilla is anti-fine dining: fancy food without the white tablecloths or the fine-dining price tag.

Greenberr

Greenberry Café

101 Regent's Park Road
London NW1 8UR

@greenberrycafe
greenberrycafe.co.uk
+44 207 483 3765

If you need a break from hectic city life, head to Primrose Hill and make time for Greenberry Café. Located on Regent's Park Road, one of the neighbourhood's prettiest streets, Greenberry is a casual all-day café capturing the area's relaxed and stylish charm. It's easy to spot thanks to its iconic green awning and the huge glass window, and when the sun's out, the outdoor tables are always buzzing. Inside, it's classic café-meets-bistro: chalkboards, exposed brick, tiled floors, and vintage furniture that gives the space its own quirky charm.

Since opening in 2012, the restaurant has earned a reputation as the go-to spot for informal breakfast and brunch among both locals and visitors to Primrose Hill. The clientele is just as you'd hope, a lovely mix of families, friends on brunch dates, and freelancers tapping away on laptops, making the most of the café's free wifi.

And the food? Greenberry serves up a vibrant, eclectic menu with seasonally inspired dishes. It's the kind of place people plan for, so arrive early or book ahead, especially if it's the weekend.

Goodbye Horses

21 Halliford Street
London N1 3HB

@goodbyehorsesldn
goodbyehorses.london

Goodbye Horses is the debut venture from Alex Young and George de Vos, part wine bar, part work of art. Tucked away in De Beauvoir and housed in a restored pub reimagined with Swiss architect Leopold Banchini, it blends the spirit of Japanese Folk Art with the elegance of English Arts and Crafts. A ten-metre bar, carved from a single oak tree, anchors the space, doubling as counter, kitchen bench and communal table. Limewashed brick, cork ceilings, and an earthen clay-and-straw floor set a warm, tactile stage for Lucy Stein's hand-painted folklore murals, which spill across a rice-paper light canopy and hessian curtains.

Seasonal small plates, from oxtail broken rice to sardine toast, pair effortlessly with a thoughtful selection of natural European wines. Food and wine are served to a backdrop of vinyl albums, handpicked daily from Goodbye Horses' extensive 4,000-plus library.

By day, the same building houses Day Trip, a pour-over coffee shop with a lush Ji-Hae Hwang-designed garden and across the street, an artisanal ice cream shop called The Dreamery opened on summer 2025.

OPENING HOURS
LUNCH
TUE-SAT 12-3
SUN 12-4
DINNER
MON-THUR 6-1030
FRI-SAT 6-11
CLOSED MON-LUNCH
+ SUNDAY DINNER

Brawn

49 Columbia Road
London E2 7RG

@brawn49
brawn.co
+44 207 729 5692

Brawn on Columbia Road in Hackney might look at first glance like your typical "East London" bistro, set in an old industrial building with low-key, vintage-inspired interiors, wooden chairs and tables, and a southern European menu often leaning Italian. But Brawn just sits a little above your average neo-bistro-meets-East-London-cool spot. It's the kind of place where, instead of ticking it off your bucket list and moving on, you think I need to come back and try the rest of the menu, because it's good—really good.

And yes, the concept is pretty much tailor-made for that East London Gen Z crowd: local seasonal produce, a menu that changes daily (with a few permanent classics, of course), and a wine list that champions excellent natural and orange wines from small producers. The menu is short but spot-on, with every dish delivering. Don't skip dessert, their panna cotta is arguably the best in London.

Since opening in 2010, Brawn has been a subtle beacon for the modern British dining scene. Nothing flashy or formal, just good food, good wine and good times.

Brawn was one of the first places in London to truly embrace the natural wine trend.

Toklas

1 Surrey Street
London WC2R 2ND

@toklas_london
toklaslondon.com
+44 203 930 8592

Just off the Strand sits Toklas, the kind of place you might want to keep secret, though London has already caught on. The name pays homage to Alice B. Toklas, writer, cookbook muse, and accidental counterculture icon for penning the first modern recipe for cannabis brownies. A fitting tribute from Amanda Sharp and Matthew Slotover, the duo behind Frieze and its orbit of art-world cool.

Toklas is part of the creative campus at 180 The Strand, the Soho House-owned brutalist landmark that now hosts exhibitions, studios, and a swirl of fashion, art, and media, yet it feels both plugged-in and self-contained. The restaurant spills into a bakery, grocery, terrace, and events space, with interiors that balance concrete edge with mid-century warmth, a kind of understated cool that's distinctly Clerkenwell-meets-West End. The real finesse comes from the menu that shifts with the seasons, turning high-quality ingredients into dishes that feel bold, unfussy, and deceptively simple.

The bakery alone is reason to stop by: still-warm loaves, glossy patisserie, generous lunch plates, and shelves stacked like a curated grocer.

Alice Toklas slipped the first cannabis brownie recipe into her 1954 cookbook, an edible footnote that helped spark the ’60s counterculture.

Toklas

St. JOHN Bread And Wine

94–96 Commercial Street
London E1 6LZ

@st.john.restaurant
stjohnrestaurant.com
+44 207 251 0848

Seen as the little sister of the original Smithfield restaurant, St. JOHN Bread and Wine is no less compelling. Opened in 2003 to house the bakery operation that had outgrown its first home, it began as a counter for loaves and takeaway wines, with a few small plates for passers-by. That didn't last long.

Soon it evolved into a full-fledged restaurant, credited with helping define East London's small-plate, seasonal dining scene. The cooking is distinctly British: unfussy, honest, and deeply satisfying. Think crisp greens, rich terrines, and what might be the city's best bacon sandwich.

Inside, the space mirrors the food, pared-back whitewashed walls, simple furniture, coat hooks, and a no-nonsense bakery counter. It's more affordable than its older sibling, yet every bit as much of a destination.

St. JOHN Smithfield

26 St. John Street
London EC1M 4AY

@st.john.restaurant
stjohnrestaurant.com
+44 207 251 0848

Opened in 1994 in a former bacon smokehouse by Smithfield Market, St. JOHN Smithfield is the original temple of nose-to-tail eating, credited for making that made bone marrow a London icon and offal cool again. Very simple interiors, no-frills surroundings. The dining room is stripped back in the best way: whitewashed walls, plain wooden furniture, nothing to pull focus from the food.

Menus change daily, but expect robust, honest British cooking, grilled meats, game, and seasonal vegetables prepared with clarity and confidence. Some dishes have become legendary, from the previous mentioned roast bone marrow with parsley salad to eccles cakes with Lancashire cheese. The wine list is as thoughtfully chosen as the menu, leaning heavily on small producers. Three decades on, St. JOHN is still both a destination and a blueprint, the kind of place that has shaped how London eats today.

Rochelle Canteen

16 Playground Gardens
London E2 7FA

@rochellecanteen
rochellecanteen.com

London has so many restaurants you could eat somewhere new every day for the rest of your life and still not make a dent. But peel back the layers and you'll find a tight-knit web behind the chaos. The truly great chefs and restaurateurs, they're all connected, collaborating, branching off, starting something new. The city's food scene isn't just big, it's a living, breathing network of talent. The story of Rochelle Canteen is no different. Like St. John, which is also interwoven in this story, many who have worked at Rochelle Canteen have now opened their own places.

Long story short: Melanie and Margot met in 1992, just before the opening of The French House Dining Room, set up by Margot, Fergus Henderson and Jon Spiteri. After Fergus and Jon left to open St. John, they ran the restaurant together until 2001, introducing event catering into the mix, working all over Britain and worldwide.

Rochelle Canteen opened in 2004, starting life with one big sharing table and a box for a till, and has gone from strength to strength over the years since, with an incredible list of people who have worked there, many of whom have now gone on to open their own places. The garden surroundings, walled off from the bustle of surrounding streets, lend peace and freshness to the Canteen.

SÓ
KI
SO
KI

Leo's Bar and Restaurant

59 Chatsworth Road
Lower Clapton
London E5 0LH

@leos.london
leosrestaurant.bar
+44 204 559 8598

On the genteel stretch of Clapton's Chatsworth Road, Leo's Bar and Restaurant is a love letter to Sardinia wrapped in mid-century Italian style. By day, it's a retro café serving expertly pulled espressos, house pastries and unfussy Italian lunches, think lasagne with crisped edges, tonnato Milanese sandwiches, or fried eggs with prosciutto and chips. Evenings shift into trattoria mode, with wood-hearth sardines, handmade pasta dusted with bottarga, and rich pork neck layered with lardo.

The space is a careful restoration of a 1960s caffe-meets-trattoria, with terrazzo floors, wood panelling, vintage vermouth posters and second-hand bentwood chairs. In the front, Formica-topped tables sit beneath a chalkboard of aperitivi; in the back, skylights flood the dining room with light. The effect is part Sophia Loren, part Wes Anderson and part Hackney local.

Come for morning coffee and a newspaper,
stay for Negronis and Sardinian pasta.

Morchella

86 Rosebery Ave
London EC1R 4QY

@morchelladining
morchelladining.co.uk
+44 207 916 0492

Morchella is a modern Mediterranean restaurant and wine bar from the team behind Newington Green favourite Perilla. Morchella has brought its refined yet easygoing style to a restored former bank just off Exmouth Market. The space is calm and minimal, with raw plaster walls, original wood panelling, and plenty of greenery, anchored by an open kitchen that encourages diners to watch the action.

The menu draws on the breadth of the Mediterranean, octopus luciana, salt-baked poussin, hake with sobrasada sauce, with produce sourced from artisanal suppliers in southern Europe and small British day boats and farms. Plates are for sharing, with a balance of precision and generosity that makes lingering inevitable. Downstairs, a private dining room hides behind the wine cellar, while outside, the terrace opens gently onto the bustle of Exmouth Market.

Morchella rides London's Med wave with modern takes on classics from Spain to Greece, served in a beautifully restored bank just off Exmouth Market.

Oma

2–4 Bedale Street
London SE1 9AL

@oma.london
oma.london
+44 208 129 6760

The wave of Italian-inspired restaurants in London has been hard to miss in recent years, but that trend may have reached its peak. Now, Greek cuisine is stepping into the spotlight, with openings like OMA leading the charge. And if you didn't make it to "trendy" Greece this summer while all your friends did, OMA might just be the next best thing.

Located in Borough Market, OMA is a sunny homage to the Greek isles and the coastal flavours surrounding them. The first-floor dining room, flooded with daylight through soaring windows, is split between a crudo bar showcasing day-boat fish and shellfish, and a live-fire kitchen where meat, fish, and vegetables meet the flames. Natural materials, soft coastal tones, and artisan-made furniture evoke the rugged Greek landscape, while the terrace bar offers year-round views over the market. The menu draws on the flavours and traditions of the Greek kitchen, combining bright, vibrant plates with heartier dishes from the hearth.

OMA is built around slow-cooked classics, seasonal at heart and made to be shared.

Noisy Oyster

2 Nicholls Clarke Yard
London E1 6SH

@noisyoyster.london
noisyoysterlondon.co.uk
+44 786 933 3701

The duo behind Soho's Firebird, Madina Kazhimova and Anna Dolgushina, are back with their latest venture: Noisy Oyster in Shoreditch. Playfully named after the tongue twister, it's not your nostalgic seaside shack but a sleek, unpretentious seafood bistro serving standout oysters, trend-setting mini martinis, and plates in a striking monochrome setting.

Inspired by Britain's seafood culture, from boat catchers to market stalls, Madina and Anna have reimagined the "bistro of the future:" stylish, upbeat, and just the right amount of rowdy.

The fish-forward menu journeys along the coasts of Italy, Spain, Portugal, and France. Oysters take centre stage, shucked to order, served bare or draped in inventive mignonettes like smoked tomato water with horseradish crème fraîche. Complementing the food are the mini martinis, perfect for sparking a meal. The "petite cocktail" trend, where quality size, striking design, and mindful drinking converge, is riding a wave across London and beyond.

Crosby Studios' design amplifies the mood. Set in the historic Norton Folgate development, the space embraces an intentional work-in-progress aesthetic: exposed ceilings, stainless steel, and reflective surfaces nodding to fishmongers' counters, softened by warm, indirect lighting.

East London vibe combined with seafood, mini-martini cocktails, and Brutalist-inspired interior design.

Sessions Arts Club

24 Clerkenwell Green
Farringdon
London EC1R 0NA

@sessionsartsclub
sessionsartsclub.com
+44 203 793 4025

Perched on the fourth floor of the historic Old Sessions House, this soaring space is anything but ordinary. A light-filled dining room framed by grand arched windows is anchored by a striking horseshoe-shaped bar and overlooked by an airy mezzanine. At its heart, you're in Clerkenwell, but in a venue that feels part restaurant, part wine bar, part art gallery, brought to life by Jonny Gent, brothers Ted and Oliver Grebelius of Sätila Studios, and architect Russell Potter of SODA Studio.

The building's heritage is honoured with stripped-back walls, raw textures, and an understated grandeur that feels distinctly Clerkenwell. In the kitchen, Florence Knight leads with quiet confidence, serving a refined, seasonal menu that nods to British, French, and Italian traditions while staying true to her love of simplicity and beautifully sourced ingredients.

@CADETLONDON / CADETL

Cadet

57 Newington Green
London N16 9PX

@cadetlondon
cadetlondon.com
+44 204 531 5302

On the edge of Newington Green, Cadet has become one of North London's most irresistible hangouts. Part wine bar, part charcutier, part cave-à-manger, it's the brainchild of wine importers Beattie and Roberts and charcutier George Jephson. And honestly, just the word charcutier should be enough to tempt you into the 30-minute trip from central London to Newington Green.

Another charming detail: the menu changes daily and is chalked up on a blackboard in true French bistro style. The charcuterie is essential, sliced to order, and desserts like beetroot with blackberries and lavender, or homemade ice cream, are worth saving room for. The wine list is excellent, featuring natural and low-intervention bottles from across Europe, and there's always something by the glass that feels like a discovery.

Half the tables are kept for walk-ins, and the room glows with old-school charm, wooden stools, hanging lamps, big windows, while in summer, a handful of outside tables turn this into the perfect place to sit with a bottle and watch Newington Green go by.

Cadet is a French wine bar on Newington Green. Very good wine, house-made charcuterie, and simple food done perfectly.

57
CADET

CAFFE
ESPRESSO
Bar Italia

Bar Italia

22 Frith Street
London W1D 4RF

@baritaliasoho
baritaliasoho.co.uk
+44 207 734 4737

Bar Italia has been a Soho institution since 1949, when Lou and Caterina Polledri first opened its doors. Tucked beneath its now-iconic neon sign, this family-run café remains at the heart of London's Italian community, now proudly overseen by the fifth generation of Polledris.

Step inside and you'll find more than just great coffee. Bar Italia is a slice of old Soho: charming, unpretentious, and full of character. Over the years, it's drawn a diverse crowd of loyal locals and famous faces alike, from David Bowie and Paul McCartney to Andrea Bocelli and Evander Holyfield.

Open daily from 7 a.m. to 3 a.m., it's a round-the-clock meeting place for early risers, night owls, and everyone in between. No wonder it's won the London Lifestyle Award for Best Café five years in a row.

Bar Italia has been Soho's unofficial living room since 1949, pouring espresso for locals and legends.

ON SALE
75 YR
ANNIVERSARY
T-SHIRTS
twist
ROCKY MARCIANO
Undefeated heavyweight champion of the world!
DON MOGARD...DECISION...10
HARRY HAFT.........KO.........3
PETE LOUTHIS.......KO.........3
TOMMY DI GORGIO..KO.........4
TED LOWRY ....DECISION...10
HAROLD MITCHELL..KO.........2
ART HENIE..........KO.........9
RED APPLEGATE..DECISION..10
REX LANE..........KO.........6
FREDDIE BESHORE..KO.........4
JOE LOUIS..........KO.........8
LEE SAVOLD.........KO.........6
GINO BUONVINO....KO.........2
BERNY REYNOLDS..KO.........3
HARRY MATTHEWS..KO.........2
JOE WOLCOTT........KO.........13
JOE WOLCOTT........KO.........1
ROLAND LA STARZA..KO.........11
EZZARD CHARLES..DECISION..15
EZZARD CHARLES...KO.........8
TKO.........9
KO.........9

SAGER +

Sager + Wilde

193 Hackney Road
London E2 8JL

@sagerandwilde
sagerandwilde.com
+44 776 116 8529

Eleven years on and Sager + Wilde is still the East London wine bar everyone wishes they'd opened first. Back in 2013, it took over a tired Victorian pub on Hackney Road and quietly rewrote the rules, ditching the white tablecloths, pouring serious wine at fair prices, and making the scene feel less like a lecture and more like a party.

The bar itself is a mood: exposed brick, soft lighting, and that now-iconic counter made from salvaged London paving stones. Behind the bar, the line-up keeps changing, grower Champagnes, new-wave naturals, Old World greats, all poured by staff who can read your mood faster than you can read the wine list.

Toasties have cult status here, and yes, you can totally drink vintage Burgundy with grilled cheese if you want. Open late, stylish but not trying too hard, Sager + Wilde still sets the tone for how a wine bar should feel, democratic, dynamic, and just the right side of decadent.

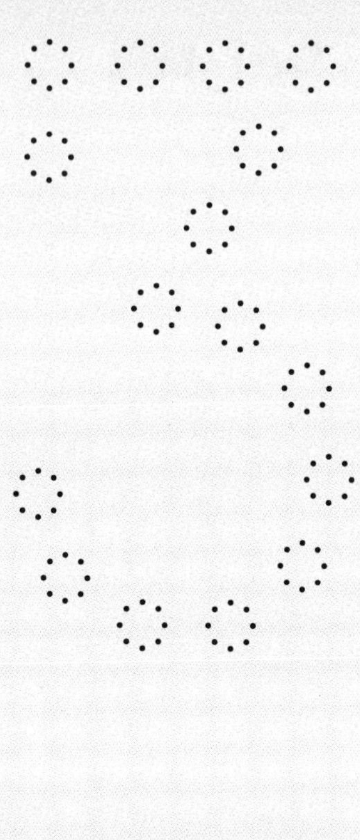

Aesop
Alex Eagle Studio
Coal Drops Yard
Dover Street Market
House of Hackney
Labour and Wait
magCulture
Margaret Howell
Perfumer H
Present & Correct
The Monocle Shop
Selfridges

Shop

Aesop

22–24 Duke of York Square
London SW3 4LY

@aesop
aesop.com
+44 207 824 8329

Aesop was founded in Melbourne in 1987 and has since become known not only for its exceptional skincare, hair, and body products, as well as its fragrances, but also for creating some of the most extraordinary concept stores in the world. Each store is a unique masterpiece, thoughtfully responding to its specific location while still expressing the brand's unmistakable design DNA. Aesop Duke of York Square in Chelsea is no exception. Designed in collaboration with the brand's long-standing partners Snøhetta, the space makes full use of its generous proportions to create bold, clearly defined forms and striking material contrasts.

Walls rendered in earthen plaster and washed in a pale rose tone echo the masonry common to this part of the city, bringing a grounded, tactile presence to the space. Materiality and palette shift subtly, rough to smooth, light to dark, creating a calm yet dynamic dialogue of contrasts.

At the centre, an existing column defines the spatial hierarchy, anchoring twelve sculptural arches that rise and curve toward the store's perimeter, dramatic, elegant, and quietly monumental. A large circular demonstration sink appears to float in space, inviting visitors to pause and engage in an Aesop product consultation.

Aesop makes stores that feel less like retail, and more like art installations you just happen to shop in.

Alex Eagle Studio

6–10 Lexington Street
London W1F 0LB

@alexeaglestudio
alexeagle.com
+44 737 599 6868

Alex Eagle has long established herself as one of London's most influential figures in fashion and interior design. With her namesake brand, Alex Eagle Studio, she's created a universe where wardrobe staples are elevated and paired with a carefully curated selection of timeless design pieces, all marked by her signature blend of understated elegance and sharp curation. She's also served as creative director for The Store X, the multi-brand retail concept with outposts in Berlin, 180 The Strand, and Soho Farmhouse.

Originally launched in a Knightsbridge townhouse, the studio now resides in a Soho loft that feels more like a home than a shop. It's a space where fashion, furniture, ceramics, rare books, and collectible design live side by side.

Beneath the shop lies the in-house tailoring studio, where the brand's Ready-to-Wear collections are handcrafted on-site. Eagle's own designs fuse British minimalism with Italian craftsmanship and a hint of French nonchalance, resulting in timeless, comfortable wardrobe essentials.

Alex Eagle personally selects all the items in the store, from furniture and design pieces to books and womenswear.

Neighbourhoods

Soho / Covent Garden / The Strand
Kings Cross / Camden / Primrose
Clerkenwell
Southwark
Chelsea / Kensington / Notting Hill
Marylebone / Fitzrovia
Shoreditch / Spitalfields
Newington Green / Dalston / Hackney

London

HAPPY
20
YEARS

A.P.C.
ba&sh

A cityscape is defined by the sum of its neighbourhoods. They are the heartbeat of a city, infusing life and diversity into its very soul. Some are artsy and vibrant, others are more serene and exclusive. Each neighbourhood has its own unique character, and we all have our favourite areas that we feel connected to. In this section, we break down the city and introduce you to the coolest neighbourhoods. All the locations in the book, along with a few bonus spots, are marked on detailed neighbourhood maps, making it easy for you to discover your favourite district.

SO

9
11
12
14
8
4
10
1
13
3
2
7
5

Soho / Covent Garden / The Strand

			Don't Miss:
1	Bar Italia (p. 115)	8	Supreme, 2-3 Peter Street, London W1F 0AA
2	Café Petiole (p. 65)	9	Adidas Original Flagship, 8 Foubert's Place, London W1F 7PD
3	Toklas (p. 83)	10	Carhartt WIP Store, 33-35 Brewer Street, London W1F 0RX
4	Alex Eagle Studio (p. 127)	11	Byredo, 40 Lexington Street, London W1F 0LN
5	Dover Street Market (p. 133)	12	Our Legacy, 1 Silver Place, London W1F 0JW
6	The Barbican (p. 161)	13	Veja, 45a Monmouth Street, London WC2H 9DG
7	National Portrait Gallery (p. 177)	14	Le Labo, 48 Monmouth Street, London WC2H 9EP

Tucked between Hyde Park and The Strand, these neighbourhoods sit side by side. And yes, it might be a stretch to group them together as one district, but each has its own distinct story and identity.

Soho hides just behind the big shopping arteries, Regent Street, Oxford Street, and Shaftesbury Avenue. Here, the pace shifts: livelier, grittier, and buzzing with energy. It's a seriously cool shopping hub, with streetwear icons like Supreme, Carhartt WIP Store and the Adidas Originals flagship alongside lifestyle favourites Byredo, Aesop, and Our Legacy, making Soho one of London's most eclectic neighbourhoods.

Covent Garden, with its famous Apple Market, has transformed into a full-blown shopping destination. Alongside the big-name brands, you'll still find independent shops, lively restaurants, and street performers keeping the area alive. Seven Dials offers a more intimate shopping scene, with cobbled streets lined with cool flagships, concept stores, and indie beauty shops.

And then there's The Strand, with Somerset House as its cultural anchor. This grand neoclassical landmark hosts exhibitions, concerts, and events year-round, and even hides the colourful Café Petiole within its walls. Just around the corner, super trendy Toklas adds its own flavour to the creative hub at 180 The Strand, serving modern Mediterranean dishes in one of London's most stylish spaces.

COVENT
TOM FORD

MARKET

4
3
1
5
8
7
2
6

Kings Cross / Camden / Primrose

			Don't miss:
1	Greenberry Café (p. 75)	5	The Lansdowne, 90 Gloucester Ave., London NW1 8HX
2	Coal Drops Yard (p. 131)	6	The Yellow Bittern, 20 Caledonian Road, London N1 9DU
3	Isokon Gallery (p. 165)	7	Chalcot Square Gardens, 8 Sharples Hall St, London NW1 8YN
4	Kenwood House (p. 167)	8	Primrose Hill, Primrose Hill Road, London NW1 4NR

Linked by one of London's most rewarding half-hour walks, Kings Cross, Camden, and their neighbours are grouped together here for good reason. Start at Kings Cross, known more for its gritty edge than its charm, it has undergone a complete transformation. Thanks to an ambitious urban renewal, especially around Coal Drops Yard, this once-overlooked area is now one of London's trendiest enclaves. It's one of my personal favourites for eating, people-watching, or just lingering over coffee. Before moving on, stop for lunch at The Yellow Bittern. Forget renewal, this is old-school: book by phone or postcard, bring cash, and expect hearty stews and pies in a setting as classic as it is controversial.

From here, follow the Regent's Canal towpath, a peaceful route that leads north to Camden. It still has a few rough edges, but that's part of the charm. It feels like a small village tucked inside the city with leafy streets, independent shops, and small cafés. Highlights include Greenberry Café and The Lansdowne, both weekend favourites, often busy with locals, and the occasional celebrity, if that's your thing.

Take a detour through Chalcot Square Gardens, a photogenic residential square that flows into Chalcot Crescent, where Paddington Bear was filmed. End the walk at Primrose Hill, a gentle rise with one of the best views across central London. If you have time, continue to Kenwood House, a lesser-known museum set in parkland. The interiors are worth a look, as is the small but impressive art collection, including Rembrandt's Self-Portrait with Two Circles.

DANGER
Men working overhead
FARA Kids
PRIMO

OSE CORNER

1
2
3
4
5
6
7

Clerkenwell

			Don't miss:
1	Morchella (p. 97)	6	Clerkenwell Close, 15 Clerkenwell Close, London EC1R 0AA
2	Sessions Arts Club (p. 109)	7	Luca, 88 St John Street, London EC1M 4EH
3	St. JOHN Smithfield (p. 89)		
4	MagCulture (p. 139)		
5	The Barbican (p. 161)		

Clerkenwell wears its history well. Once known as London's 'Little Italy', a nod to the influx of Italian immigrants in the 19th and 20th centuries, the area still carries a certain old-world charisma, though these days it's more espresso bar than Catholic grotto. Its architectural patchwork is part of the appeal: Georgian townhouses, Victorian warehouses, and sharp contemporary builds coexist in that distinctly London way, layered, lived-in, and photogenic. Look out for 15 Clerkenwell Close, a striking modern limestone building by architect Amin Taha that sparked debate, yet now stands as a bold statement of how old and new can meet.

It's not just pretty façades. Clerkenwell is one of the most densely populated creative hubs on the planet, with more architects and design studios per square mile than anywhere else. Each spring, Clerkenwell Design Week turns the neighbourhood into a global showcase, with makers, thinkers, and design devotees descending on its storied venues.

Much of the area's industrial past has been reimagined, former factories now house loft apartments, brand showrooms, or low-lit wine bars. The food scene in Clerkenwell is a mix of cosy pubs, neighbourhood favourites, and destination restaurants hidden in its maze of alleys. Cultural credentials are strong too, with the Brutalist Barbican nearby as a defining highlight.

5
3
6
4
7
8
2
1

Southwark

			Don't Miss:
1	Art'otel London Battersea Power Station (p. 17)	6	Borough Market, 8 Southwark Street, London SE1 1TL
2	Bermonds Locke (p. 21)	7	Fashion and Textile Museum, 83 Bermondsey Street, London SE1 3XF
3	The Hoxton Southwark (p. 41)	8	The Gladstone Arms, 64 Lant Street, London SE1 1QN
4	Oma (p. 101)		
5	Tate Modern (p. 187)		

Southwark, just south of the Thames, covers the stretch known as the South Bank, from Tate Modern to London Bridge. It's one of the most atmospheric riverside walks in the city, lined with brutalist landmarks, glassy new builds, and centuries-old pubs.

Historically, this was London's unruly playground. Just beyond the reach of the City's laws, Southwark was where people went to drink, gamble, and watch theatre, think raucous taverns, bawdy plays, and more than a few questionable establishments.

Today, the area has undergone a complete transformation. Old warehouses now house art galleries, design studios, and sleek restaurants. The creative energy is strong, especially around Borough Market, where food culture meets history in full force.

Tate Modern, one of the world's most visited art museums, is a must, both for its exhibitions and its panoramic views. Further west, Battersea Power Station has also reopened after a dramatic redevelopment, transforming the old industrial giant into a new cultural and retail destination. Southwark is a fascinating mix of grit and gloss, where London's past and future meet along the riverfront.

12
13
14
8
9
15
5
4
6
7
10
11
1
2
3

Chelsea / Kensington / Notting Hill

			Don't miss:
1	Lime Tree Hotel (p. 29)	10	Granger & Co., 237-239 Pavilion Road, London SW1X 0BP
2	Common Breads (p. 55)	11	Ottolenghi, 261 Pavilion Road, London SW1X 0BP
3	Aesop (p. 123)	12	Canteen, 310 Portobello Road, London W10 5TA
4	Leighton House (p. 169)	13	Holy Carrot, 156 Portobello Road, London W11 2EB
5	Serpentine Gallery (p. 183)	14	Notting Hill Bakery, 283 Westbourne Grove, London W11 2QA
6	The Design Museum (p. 189)	15	Supermarket of Dreams, 126 Holland Park Ave, London W11 4UE
7	Victoria and Albert Museum (p. 191)		
8	The Lost Poet (p. 45)		
9	Kuro Coffee (p. 59)		

Chelsea, Kensington and Notting Hill sit side by side in London's more exclusive west. These neighbourhoods represent a calm, refined elegance with townhouses tucked into leafy backstreets, just a few steps from glamorous shopping avenues. At the centre sits Sloane Square, Chelsea's beating heart, where cafés, restaurants and independent shops cluster.

The so-called Museum Mile strings together icons like the V&A, the Serpentine, the Design Museum and the jewel-box Leighton House.

Notting Hill has a different vibe. It's a lived-in neighbourhood where real people go about their everyday lives. Like Chelsea and Kensington, it's also a fashionable part of town, known for its quaint houses, especially the colourful ones along Portobello Road, and the iconic Portobello Road Market, packed with everything from antiques to vintage clothes and street food. There's a distinct village-like atmosphere here, and locals genuinely love their community.

MICHELIN
BIBENDUM
MICHELIN TYRE CIE

LUNCH,
COCKTAILS

8
10
3
12
5
7
11
13
9
1
4
6

Marylebone / Fitzrovia

1 Inhabit Southwick Street (p. 25)
2 The Newman (p. 47)
3 Labour and Wait (p. 137)
4 Margaret Howell (p. 141)
5 Perfumer H (p. 143)
6 Selfridges (p. 155)
7 The Monocle Shop (p. 151)
8 Lisson Gallery (p. 173)

Don't Miss:

9 St. JOHN Marylebone, 98 Marylebone Lane, London W1U 2QA
10 Avobar, 60 Chiltern Street, London W1U 7RB
11 The Monocle Café, 18 Chiltern Street, London W1U 7QA
12 Anna & Nina, 54 Chiltern Street, London W1U 7QX
13 Granger & Co, 105 Marylebone High Street, London W1U 4RS

Marylebone and Fitzrovia sit side by side and share a similar vibe, but Marylebone has the edge when it comes to style. It's undoubtedly one of the most fashionable neighbourhoods in London. Marylebone's small community of shopkeepers, craftspeople, and independent brands is a chic and civilised contrast to the crowded, busy Oxford Street. That said, make a quick stop at Selfridges, arguably London's best department store, but skip the chaos of Oxford Street and head straight for the elegant, tree-lined calm of Marylebone High Street. It's a haven for food lovers, home to some of London's best restaurants. Don't miss the newest outpost of St. JOHN and, of course, the celebrity magnet Chiltern Firehouse on nearby Chiltern Street (currently closed for renovation).

If you're staying over, check in at the cosy, wellness-focused Inhabit Southwick Street. The handsome red-brick buildings of Chiltern Street and neighbouring Dorset Street are worth a detour, lined with carefully curated spots like Labour and Wait, The Monocle Shop, and Perfumer H, each offering its own take on understated luxury. Over on Wigmore Street, the Margaret Howell flagship store is not to be missed.

Fitzrovia, just east of Marylebone, has a few low-key gems of its own. Pop into The Newman for a drink or a stay, and don't miss Lisson Gallery, one of the capital's most respected contemporary art spaces, just a short walk northwest of Marylebone High Street. And when it's time for a culture break, the Wallace Collection awaits, a beautiful, free museum housed in a historic townhouse, complete with an excellent courtyard café.

34
M

OCLE
54
ROOM THIRTY
MONOCLE
Read
Listen
Wear: MONOCLE
MONOCLE
New Shop.
New Season.
New Look.
Marylebone
AIR

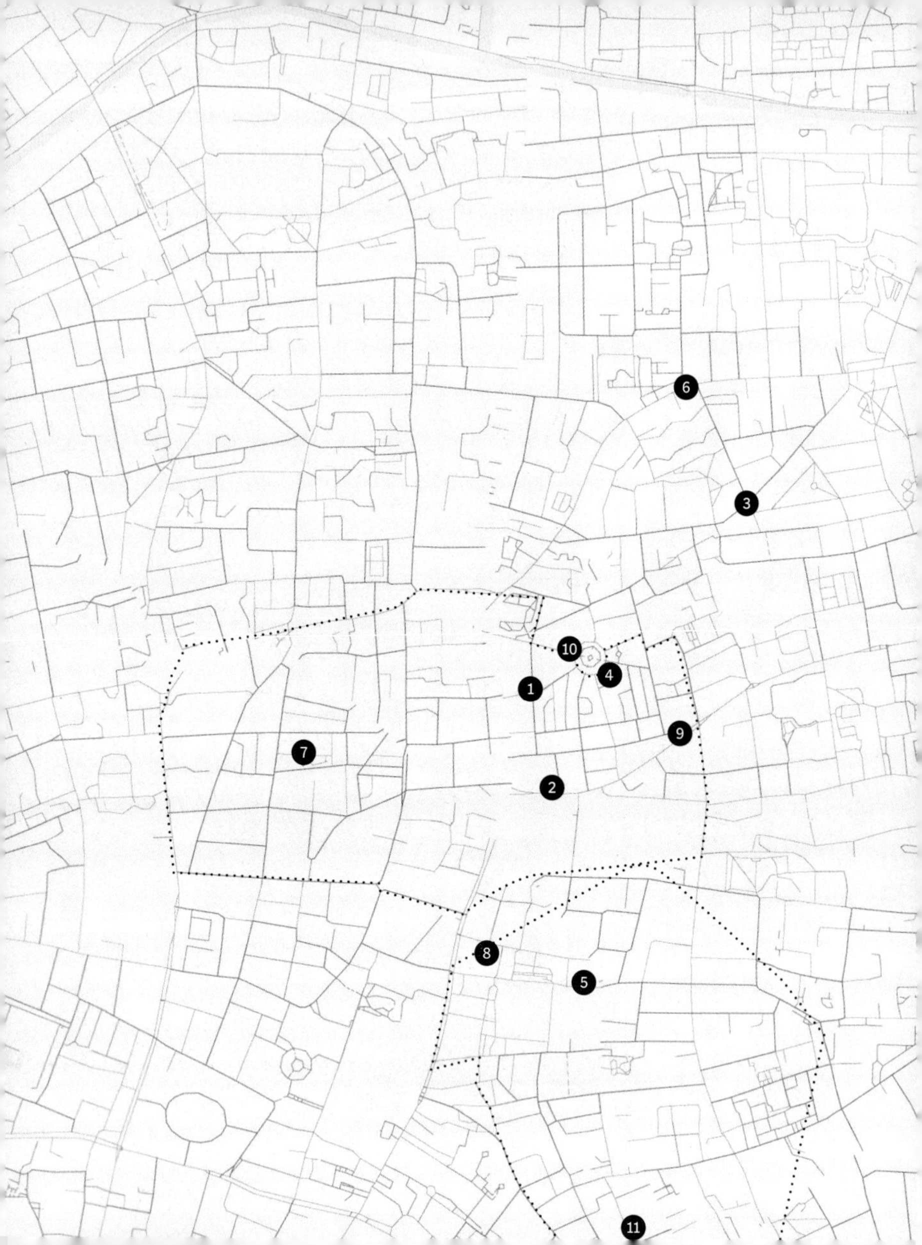

6
3
10
4
1
9
7
2
8
5
11

Shoreditch / Spitalfields

			Don't Miss:
1	One Hundred Shoreditch (p. 33)	8	Dennis Severs' House, 18 Folgate Street, London E1 6BX
2	Shoreditch House (p. 37)	9	Shoreditch Fish and Chips, 117 Redchurch Street, London E2 7DL
3	Brawn (p. 79)	10	Leila's Shop, Calvert Ave, Bethnal Green, London E2 7JP
4	Rochelle Canteen (p. 91)	11	Ara Restaurant, 1 New Drum Street, London E1 7AY
5	St JOHN Bread and Wine (p. 87)		
6	Sager + Wilde (p. 119)		
7	House of Hackney (p. 135)		

East London begins just beyond Liverpool Street Station, and the contrast hits instantly. This is the city's creative engine room, where two neighbouring districts offer two very different takes on cool. Shoreditch is all grit and swagger. It's the kind of place where a former warehouse might house a concept gallery, a start-up hub, or a subterranean bar, often all three. Redchurch Street and Curtain Road are the main arteries, lined with fashion labels, curated interiors, and cafés where the filter coffee comes with a side of attitude. Book lunch at Rochelle Canteen (hidden in an old schoolyard), check in at One Hundred Shoreditch, and browse the maximalist world of House of Hackney.

Just south, Spitalfields is more composed, but no less compelling. Built on layers of immigration and industry, it's a pocket of London where Huguenot townhouses meet modern market stalls and Bengali curry houses. The iconic Old Spitalfields Market is the beating heart, but make time for cult favourites too: St. JOHN Bread and Wine, oysters and mini martinis at the new Noisy Oyster, or the immersive time capsule that is Dennis Severs' House.

TRUMAN

11
5
6
2
1
10
9
7
8
4
3

Newington Green / Dalston / Hackney

			Don't Miss:
1	Jolene Bakery & Restaurant (p. 53)	7	Hector, 49a Ardleigh Road, London N1 4HS
2	Cadet (p. 111)	8	Lardo, Unit 3, 201 Richmond Road, London E8 3NJ
3	Café Cecilia (p. 61)	9	Oeno Maris, 105 Newington Green Road, London N1 4QY
4	Goodbye Horses (p. 77)	10	Stella's, 101 Newington Green Road, London N1 4QY
5	Leo's Bar and Restaurant (p. 93)	11	Primeur, Barnes Motors, 116 Petherton Road, London N5 2RT
6	Perilla (p. 71)		

Welcome to the quieter, cooler corner of northeast London, a patchwork of neighbourhoods that each bring their own flavour, from babycino parks to late-night wine bars.

Newington Green is leafy and low-key. Once a radical hotspot for dissenters and philosophers, it's now better known for posh pizza, designer prams, and excellent restaurants. Perilla does modern British fine dining without the fuss, Cadet brings the natural wine crowd, and Jolene is the place for a long, flour-dusted breakfast. Check out Oeno Maris (fishmonger–wine bar) or Stella's (butcher–listening bar), old-school shop concepts with a gen-z hipster edge.

Swing south and things get livelier. Hackney isn't just hipster territory; it's a whole borough of contrasts. London Fields and Hackney Central are packed on sunny weekends, full of cafés, pubs, and that certain East London energy. Highlights include Café Cecilia on the canal and Leo's on Chatsworth Road, both neighbourhood favourites with cult local followings.

And then there's Dalston, grittier, gayer, and still clinging to its late-night soul. The high street has changed, but the energy is intact. Check out Hector's, a cosy natural wine bar, and Climpson & Sons, their coffee roastery just a few minutes' walk away. Dalston is less polished than its neighbours, but that's exactly the point.

SECOM
ALTER

Coal Drops Yard

Stable Street
London N1C 4DQ

@coaldropsyard
kingscross.co.uk/coal-drops-yard

London has spent the past decade perfecting the art of adaptive reuse, reviving old structures and injecting them with new energy. The Shard and Battersea Power Station are just two examples of how the city's architectural past keeps evolving. Coal Drops Yard is part of this same movement and plays a central role in the broader urban renewal of the King's Cross area.

Originally built in the mid-1800s, the two-storey brick and cast-iron structures were used to transfer coal from train wagons to horse-drawn carts, with shipments arriving from mines in Northern England.

In 2018, the site was reimagined by Heatherwick Studio and reopened to the public as a dynamic, culturally vibrant destination. Independent galleries, niche retailers, and experimental restaurants moved into the old coal depot, transforming it into a creative hub at the heart of the capital.

Today, Coal Drops Yard is home to a curated mix of fashion, lifestyle, design, and beauty. You'll find brands like Universal Works, A.P.C., The Sports Edit, Paul Smith, Aesop, COS, & Other Stories, Carhartt WIP, Kitchen Provisions, Uniqlo, and many more.

Dover Street Market

18–22 Haymarket
London SW1Y 4DG

@doverstreetmarketlondon
london.doverstreetmarket.com
+44 207 518 0680

Dover Street Market is a fashion institution conceived by Comme des Garçons founder Rei Kawakubo and her long-time partner, Adrian Joffe. The concept first opened its doors in London's Mayfair back in 2004, with the aim of creating a space where fashion, art, and culture could collide, a "beautiful chaos" where boundaries dissolve and creativity takes centre stage.

Now located in a former Burberry building on Haymarket, DSM London remains the retail headquarters of an international empire that now spans Tokyo, New York, Los Angeles, Singapore, Beijing, and Paris. It was here in London that, that Kawakubo's radical retail vision took shape, each floor a curated maze of installations, designer capsules, and unexpected collaborations. It's the kind of place where Comme des Garçons sits alongside Gucci, Craig Green, Bode and a vintage Rolex counter.

For Kawakubo and Joffe, DSM has always been about more than fashion. It's a home for creative misfits, a space where risk is rewarded, and contradictions are welcome. Paris, once dismissed by Joffe as "undeserving," now has two DSM offshoots. Because in this world, the rules are meant to be rewritten.

A TALE OF INTERIORS

House of Hackney

St Michael's Clergy
House, Mark Street
London EC2A 4ER

@houseofhackney
houseofhackney.com
+44 207 739 3901

Tucked away in Shoreditch, House of Hackney's flagship store at St Michael's offers a bold reinterpretation of the British interiors boutique. Set within a restored 1856 clergy house, the four-storey space, launched in 2011, is an immersive exploration of the brand's maximalist aesthetic, where Victorian Gothic and Arts & Crafts meet 1970s eclecticism.

Founded by Frieda Gormley and Javvy Royle, House of Hackney began as a personal design mission. The couple were on the hunt for bold, botanical-inspired interiors to bring their East London home to life. When they couldn't find what they were looking for, they simply made it themselves. What started as a creative workaround soon blossomed into a brand known for its romantic take on British design and unwavering commitment to sustainability.

Each room has been styled as a domestic interior, allowing visitors to move through spaces layered with richly patterned textiles, sculptural lighting, and saturated colour palettes. Highlights include custom Axminster carpets, a curated display of emerging artist work, and the brand's own richly pigmented paint range.

STANLEY
STANLEY

Labour and Wait

48 Dorset Street
London W1U 7NE

@labourandwait
labourandwait.co.uk
+44 207 729 6253

Step into Labour and Wait, and you step into a world where function and form coexist in quiet harmony. Founded in 2000 by two former menswear designers disillusioned with fast-paced fashion cycles, the store was born out of a desire to champion timeless, utilitarian objects made to last. What began in a tiny Cheshire Street shop in East London, open only on weekends, has since grown into an institution, with a flagship on Redchurch Street, a Marylebone outpost, and even locations in Tokyo and Dover Street Market outpost.

The aesthetic is pared-back but deeply evocative. Think enamel soap dishes, Japanese dustpans, Welsh wool blankets, French soap flakes, and Kaweco fountain pens presented with reverence. Each object is chosen not just for its beauty, but for its purpose, a return to the kind of buying that feels deliberate, almost moral. The founders have spent years sourcing from specialist makers around the world, many of whom still produce goods the old-fashioned way.

This is slow retail, steeped in an Arts and Crafts ethos and reimagined for the modern world. In a landscape flooded with disposables, Labour and Wait offers something authentic: real things, honestly made. A reminder that good design isn't about novelty, it's about longevity.

MAGCULTURE
270 St
MONOCLE
MONOCLE
MONOCLE
MONOCLE
MAGCULTURE
MAGCULTURE
DESIRED LANDSCAPES
CAKE ZINE
DADA
magCulture.com

magCulture

270 St John Street
London EC1V 4PE

@magculture
magculture.com
+44 203 759 8022

What began as a blog and a bold declaration, "We love magazines" has evolved into a physical shrine for print lovers. Housed in a former newsagent's on St John Street, magCulture Shop has become the beating heart of London's indie magazine scene. With more than 700 titles displayed on sleek Vitsoe shelving systems, it's part gallery, part archive, and entirely fuelled by passion.

Clerkenwell wasn't a random pick, it's just down the road from where The Gentleman's Magazine coined the very term in 1731. A fitting coincidence, as this space bridges past, present, and future in editorial design. From cult indie gems to globally admired design titles, every magazine is chosen with the same care and intention as its makers.

And at a time when digital fatigue is real and the analogue revival is gaining ground, magCulture feels especially relevant. Real magazines, tactile, slow, and beautifully made, are no longer niche; they're a growing market and a deliberate choice. A counterpoint to screen time and algorithm-fed content.

MagCulture is also a working studio, consultancy, and creative nerve centre for all things print. Expect talks, events, pop-ups, curated deliveries, and a journal that reads like a love letter to the printed page.

Margaret Howell

34 Wigmore Street
London W1U 2RS

@margarethowellltd
margarethowell.co.uk
+44 207 009 9009

Classic British fashion can sometimes feel, well, classic in a more conservative sense, but Margaret Howell proves it doesn't have to be. Her aesthetic is grounded in tradition, yet quietly radical, especially through her MHL line, where workwear references are refined into clean, considered silhouettes that feel both utilitarian and elegant.

It all started with one shirt. In the early 1970s, Howell came across a perfectly worn-in 1920s pinstripe shirt at a jumble sale. That single piece sparked her signature menswear-led style, tailored, timeless, and rooted in craftsmanship. She opened her first shop on South Molton Street in 1976, and when she noticed women were buying the clothes for themselves, she expanded into womenswear. Her flagship on Wigmore Street, designed in collaboration with architect William Russell, is more than just a retail space. It's part gallery, part studio, a calm, curated world where her clothing sits alongside ceramics, books, and mid-century modern furniture. It also plays host to exhibitions celebrating British design classics, from Ercol to Anglepoise. Today, Margaret Howell is sold worldwide with 12 own shops in Europe, over 100 outlets in Japan and an established online business.

PERFUMER H
LEATHER
PERFUMER H
SMOKE

Perfumer H

19 Chiltern Street
London W1U 7PH

@perfumerhlondon
perfumerh.com
+44 203 336 7350

Originally conceptualised as a temporary pop-up, Perfumer H at 19 Chiltern Street has evolved into a quietly essential fixture, rooted deeply in the character of its vibrant Marylebone surroundings.

Created by Lyn Harris, one of the world's most respected perfumers, the space evokes the quiet elegance of an old-world apothecary blended with the practicality of a utilitarian grocer, mirroring the ethos of the street's carefully curated independent shops.

Inside, you'll find a considered edit of unconventional fragrances for self and space, alongside candles, pantry goods, and sensory delights designed to elevate the everyday. Harris imagined a space filled with her personal essentials, created in collaboration with like-minded artisans. She partnered with a master glassblower, designer, and architect to ensure every detail feels tactile and intentional. All bottles and vessels are hand-blown and engraved by glass artist Michael Ruh, with the option to personalise in gold. The boutiques are styled in natural wood, metal, and glass, spaces that are refined, quiet, and unmistakably personal.

Blending apothecary charm with artisan craft, Perfumer H captures the spirit of Chiltern Street.

PRESENT /&/ CORRECT

Present & Correct

12 Bury Place
London WC1A 2JL

@presentandcorrect
presentandcorrect.com
+44 207 242 1421

If you're into old-school stationery, vintage finds, and the quiet joy of a freshly sharpened pencil, you're not alone. In a world ruled by screens, social feeds, and 24/7 digital noise, analogue objects like pens, notebooks, and paperclips are staging a quiet but meaningful comeback.

And nowhere captures that quiet revival better than Present & Correct. Set in a heritage unit in Bloomsbury, just steps from the British Museum, this beautifully restrained shop is a treasure trove of desk essentials and design oddities. Founded by two graphic designers with a lifelong obsession with stationery, Present & Correct started online in 2009 before opening its first physical store in Clerkenwell. The new location, designed by Architecture for London, is a study in minimalism: maple plywood, ash timber, and Vitsœ shelving arranged in a grid inspired by the ISO paper sizing chart.

Inside, everything is curated with care: stamps, brass paperclips, vintage calligraphy sets, Japanese notebooks, graph-paper socks, and wooden tape dispensers. Some items are designed in-house, others unearthed on sourcing trips across Europe and Asia. But all of it shares the same quiet mission, to spark a distant memory, make you smile, or see the mundane in a new light.

In an age of digital fatigue, Present & Correct offers the joy of analogue treasures, a place where retro stationery feels like the future.

7
14
21
28
35

55.-
125.-
225.-
35.-
MONOCLE
30.-
325.-
160.-

The Monocle Shop

34 Chiltern Street
London W1U 7QH

@ shop.monocle
monocle.com
+44 207 486 8770

Tucked into the independent charm of Chiltern Street, The Monocle Shop is a natural extension of the magazine's world, smart, stylish, and quietly cosmopolitan. Inside, you'll find a refined selection of travel accessories, elegant stationery, exclusive collaborations, and the full library of Monocle books and back issues, all curated for those with a global eye and an appreciation for craftsmanship.

Founded in 2007 by Tyler Brûlé, Monocle magazine has built a loyal following with its blend of global affairs, design, culture, and retail, always with a focus on quality over trends. That same ethos permeates the shop, where everything has purpose and nothing feels rushed.

Just a few doors down, The Monocle Café offers another slice of the brand's lifestyle vision. Compact, polished, and distinctly Tokyo-meets-Scandi in feel, it's the perfect spot for a well-brewed flat white, a bento-style lunch, or simply catching up on the latest issue

The Monocle Shop is Chiltern Street's global outpost, a brick-and-mortar distillation of the magazine itself.

MONOCLE
34
34
Read MONOCLE
Read
Listen
Wear MONOCLE
MONOCLE
New Shop
New Season
New Look

Selfridges

400 Oxford Street
London W1A 1AB

@ theofficialselfridges
selfridges.com
+44 207 160 6222

London has no shortage of department stores, from Liberty with its iconic Tudor revival building to Harrods, the undisputed giant of Knightsbridge. Each offers its own version of luxury and spectacle. But when it comes to setting trends, one name stands out: Selfridges.

It isn't the largest, nor does it have Liberty's romantic architecture, yet Selfridges leads the way in how we experience shopping today. This is where retail feels dynamic and forward-looking. Expect seasonal campaigns that go far beyond window displays, curated fashion and beauty edits, innovative food halls and wellness spaces, and in-store experiences that often feel more like exhibitions than simple shopping trips.

Over the years, Selfridges has established itself as Europe's most trend-conscious department store, regularly introducing ideas and experiences that other retailers later adopt. Whether you come for the fashion, the food, or simply to see what's next, Selfridges offers a snapshot of modern London at its most creative.

At Selfridges, fashion, food, and culture aren't just sold, they're actually setting the trends.

SELFRIDGE
& Co
LIMITED

The Barbican
Isokon Gallery
Kenwood House
Leighton House
Lisson Gallery
National Portrait Gallery
Sadie Coles HQ
Serpentine Gallery
Tate Modern
The Design Museum
Victoria and Albert Museum

Explore

The Barbican

Silk Street
London EC2Y 8DS

@barbicancentre
barbican.org.uk
+44 207 870 2500

A Brutalist landmark and "city within a city," the Barbican blends homes, gardens and one of Europe's most ambitious arts centres. The Barbican is London's ultimate Brutalist icon. A bold concrete experiment that reimagined how a city could live, work and play. Designed by Chamberlin, Powell and Bon on a site devastated by the Blitz, the idea was radical: a city within a city, lifted above street level, blending homes, schools, gardens, a church and one of Europe's most ambitious arts centres.

The architecture is often labelled Brutalist, but the influences go far beyond raw concrete. Roman fortresses, French Modernism, Mediterranean terraces and even medieval urban planning shaped its form. Forty-storey towers, sweeping highwalks, a lake, and London's second-largest Conservatory form an unexpected tropical oasis hovering above the theatre's fly tower.

Inside, the Barbican Centre is home to the London Symphony Orchestra, international concerts, cutting-edge exhibitions at The Curve and Barbican Art Gallery, and a busy programme of design, film, photography and performance. Its foyers double as lively public spaces animated by installations and live music, making it as much a civic hub as an arts destination.

Since opening in 1982, the Barbican has stayed true to its vision: a modernist dream of urban living and culture that still feels futuristic today.

Isokon Gallery

Lawn Road
London NW3 2XD

@isokongallery
isokongallery.org
+44 771 350 7018

Once the garage of London's most modern apartment block, the Isokon Gallery is now a quietly compelling design destination in Hampstead. Tucked beneath the Grade I-listed Isokon Building, also known as the Lawn Road Flats, the gallery tells the story of a radical experiment in urban living that became the epicentre of North London's avant-garde during the 1930s and 1940s. Designed in 1934 by Wells Coates for visionary couple Jack and Molly Pritchard (both specialists in plywood), the building was home to some of the era's most progressive minds. Walter Gropius, Marcel Breuer, Agatha Christie, Paul Nash and even a few suspected spies all passed through its curved concrete corridors.

The gallery itself, realised in 2014, was spearheaded by Magnus Englund, who lives in the penthouse and restored it to its original plywood-clad glory. Together with Fiona Lamb and Avanti Architects, Englund transformed the long-abandoned garage into a museum-like space filled with period furniture, architectural drawings, rare photographs, and iconic pieces from the Isokon furniture line, think Marcel Breuer's Long Chair and Egon Riss's Penguin Donkey.

The gallery is open on weekends from March to November.

Kenwood House

Hampstead Lane
London NW3 7JR

@kenwood_house_hampstead_heath
english-heritage.org.uk/visit/places/kenwood
+44 208 348 1286

On the edge of Hampstead Heath, wrapped in landscaped gardens that shift with the seasons, sits Kenwood House, one of London's best-kept secrets. This elegant 18th-century villa hides an impressive art collection, including Rembrandt's Self-Portrait with Two Circles.

Inside, the noise of the city fades. Sunlight spills into classical rooms where refined plasterwork meets a quietly domestic charm. The collection spans from Gainsborough and Vermeer to Turner, Reynolds and Romney, the kind of line-up that could fill a small museum, yet here it feels intimate, almost personal.

But Kenwood isn't just for the art crowd. It's for families with picnic blankets, solo wanderers in need of green space, and anyone who fancies a coffee with a view. The lawns are made for slow strolls or lazy afternoons, while Humphry Repton's landscaped gardens frame the house in a perfect mix of woodland, water and open meadow.

It's only a few miles from the centre, yet it feels worlds away, offering a rare blend of culture, nature and calm you'll want to come back to.

Leighton House

12 Holland Park Road
London W14 8LZ

@leightonsambournemuseums
rbkc.gov.uk/museums
+44 207 361 3783

London has no shortage of museums. The blockbuster ones pull in millions each year, and in summer you'll likely spend more time in the queue than in the galleries. Luckily, there are alternatives, the historic private homes turned museums, where the crowds thin and the character deepens.

Leighton House in Kensington is one of the best. The artist Sir Frederic Leighton (1830–1896) spent three decades turning a modest villa into an architectural manifesto, a stage set of art, objects, and daring ideas.

The showstopper is the Arab Hall, with its golden dome, Venetian mosaics, and tiles imported from Damascus. There's also the Silk Room, hung with works by Millais, Sargent, and Alma-Tadema, plus charming oddities everywhere you look; hidden chimneys, oversized passageways, and more than 80 of Leighton's own paintings.

Fresh from a major restoration in 2022, the house once again feels like a living portrait of the artist's taste. Add in a café and garden, and it's as much a serene retreat as it is a museum.

Spandau Ballet's 1983 hit 'Gold' turned Leighton House's Arab Hall into a pop video icon.

Lisson Gallery

27 Bell Street
London NW1 5BY

@lisson_gallery
www.lissongallery.com
+44 207 724 2739

Lisson Gallery isn't just another white cube, it's one of the world's most influential stages for contemporary art. Founded in 1967 by Nicholas Logsdail, it helped launch the careers of Minimalist and Conceptual heavyweights like Donald Judd, Sol LeWitt, and Richard Long, while giving early space to British sculptors such as Anish Kapoor and Tony Cragg. Over the decades, the roster has only expanded, Marina Abramović, Ai Weiwei, and John Akomfrah all call it home, alongside a fresh new generation redefining what art can be. Today, with outposts in London, New York, Los Angeles, Shanghai and Beijing, Lisson continues to shape the conversation, proving that half a century in, it's still setting the pace.

Lisson began almost by accident in 1967 with a student squat show that nearly sold out, the rest is history.

MAGICK

NATIONAL PORTRAIT GALLE

National Portrait Gallery

St. Martin's Place
London WC2H 0HE

@nationalportraitgallery
npg.org.uk
+44 207 306 0055

Just off Trafalgar Square, the National Portrait Gallery tells Britain's story through faces, kings, queens, rebels and icons. Where else can you meet Henry VIII, Elizabeth I, Shakespeare, Churchill, Adele, and even Harry Styles, all in one afternoon? Fresh from a major 2023 revamp, the galleries are brighter, sharper, and, as with most UK museums, free to visit.

Founded in 1856, it's home to some of the country's most recognisable images: Shakespeare's enigmatic Chandos Portrait, Hilliard's jewel-like Elizabeth I, and Graham Sutherland's brutal take on Churchill. The roll call of artists is equally stellar, from van Dyck and Reynolds to Hockney and Rankin.

The collection skips easily between Tudor pomp, Regency polish, and contemporary photography, serving up a crash course in British history where personality matters as much as politics. And with rotating exhibitions and new commissions, there's always a fresh face to discover.

David Hockney painted Harry Styles in May 2022 during a portrait session at his Normandy studio.

Sadie Coles HQ

Sadie Coles HQ

62 Kingly Street
London W1B 5QN

8 Bury Street
London SW1Y 6AB

@sadiecoleshq
sadiecoles.com
+44 207 493 8611

Since opening in 1997 with a debut that paired John Currin's paintings with Sarah Lucas's offsite installation The Law, Sadie Coles HQ has been at the forefront of London's contemporary art scene. Representing over fifty established and emerging artists from around the world, the gallery has never been tied to one formula or one address.

Over the years, it has worked from multiple spaces across the city, mixing high-profile shows with more experimental off-site projects and international collaborations. In Soho, The Shop at Kingly Street doubles as a platform for young galleries, curators and live events under the GARGLE programme. The St James's space, opened in 2021, brings a different kind of intimacy to the programme, while autumn 2025 will see the launch of a six-storey Georgian townhouse on Savile Row in Mayfair.

Whether showing global names or giving a stage to new voices, Sadie Coles HQ has built its reputation on keeping the conversation moving and keeping London's art world on its toes.

Serpentine Galleries

Kensington Gardens
London W2 3XA

@serpentineuk
serpentinegalleries.org
+44 207 402 6075

Tucked into Kensington Gardens, the Serpentine Galleries may be modest in size, but their influence stretches far beyond. Free to visit and firmly focused on the cutting edge, they've staged shows with names from Marina Abramović to Damien Hirst, all while keeping the dialogue around contemporary art sharp and surprising.

Since 2000, their annual Pavilion commission has turned the lawn into London's most exciting architectural playground. Each summer, a world-renowned architect, new to building in the UK, creates a temporary structure that's part sculpture, part social space, and always a talking point. Zaha Hadid launched the series, with later contributions by Frank Gehry, Herzog & de Meuron with Ai Weiwei, Bjarke Ingels, Sou Fujimoto, and Francis Kéré. For a few months, it becomes one of the city's most photographed landmarks before disappearing like a mirage.

The galleries themselves are split between Serpentine South, a light-filled neoclassical building, and Serpentine North, a 19th-century structure extended with a fluid, futuristic wing designed by Zaha Hadid.

The original Serpentine Gallery is housed in a former teahouse, serving up cutting-edge art instead of Earl Grey.

Tate Modern

Bankside
London SE1 9TG

@tate
tate.org.uk
+44 207 887 8888

Housed in the former Bankside Power Station, Tate Modern is a cathedral of contemporary art. Its vast Turbine Hall alone is worth the visit. Since opening in 2000, Tate Modern has transformed the South Bank into a cultural destination, drawing millions each year to see one of the world's most important collections of modern and contemporary works.

The museum's free permanent displays span from early 20th-century pioneers to today's most influential artists, with big names like Picasso, Rothko, Hockney and Bourgeois sitting alongside bold new voices. Temporary exhibitions, often ticketed, dominate the headlines, from immersive installations to large-scale retrospectives. One of the defining moments in its history came in 2003, when Olafur Eliasson's "The Weather Project" bathed the Turbine Hall in the glow of an artificial sun, drawing over two million visitors and cementing the museum's reputation for ambitious, transformative works.

The 2016 addition of the Blavatnik Building expanded the gallery space by 60 per cent, introducing new performance areas, intimate viewing rooms and a 360-degree terrace with some of London's best skyline views.

DESIGN

The Design Museum

224–238 Kensingtion
High Street, London W8 6AG

@designmuseum
designmuseum.org
+44 203 862 5900

From its industrial beginnings in a converted banana warehouse on Shad Thames to its current Kensington landmark, the Design Museum has always been London's temple to design in all its forms.

Between 1989 and 2016, its riverside galleries hosted smart, stylish shows on everyone from Zaha Hadid and Dieter Rams to Christian Louboutin and Thomas Heatherwick, cementing its reputation as the place where design meets culture.

Since 2016, the museum has occupied a modernist icon on Kensington High Street. Its dramatic concrete roof and distinctive façade were restored by OMA, Allies and Morrison, and Arup, while John Pawson carved out serene, light-filled interiors wrapped around a soaring oak-lined atrium. Free permanent displays sit alongside major blockbusters, drawing nearly a million visitors a year.

Victoria And Albert Museum + V&A East

Cromwell Road
London SW7 2RL

V&A East Storehouse
Parkes Street, Queen Elizabeth
Olympic Park, Hackney Wick
London E20 3AX

@vamuseum
vam.ac.uk
+44 207 942 2000

Few museums capture creativity on such a grand scale as the V&A. Founded in 1852 and renamed in honour of Queen Victoria and Prince Albert in 1899, it has become one of the world's great collections of art and design. Its South Kensington home is a warren of galleries where fashion, photography, ceramics, jewellery and furniture chart 5,000 years of human imagination, all wrapped in some of London's most beautiful Victorian architecture.

But the V&A is far from stuck in the past. Out east, in Stratford's Queen Elizabeth Olympic Park, V&A East is reinventing what a museum can be. First came the Storehouse, designed by Diller Scofidio + Renfro, where you can wander through the museum's vast back-of-house collections, usually hidden from view. The flagship V&A East Museum will follow in 2026, anchoring a new cultural quarter alongside Sadler's Wells East.

V&A East proofs that Britain's grandest institutions can still lead the way forward.

WESTON COLLECTIONS HALL

Index

45
17
34
KINGS CROSS / CAMDEN /
48
37
40
42
9
3
39
MARYLEBONE / FITZRO
43
33
30
8
SOHO / COVENT GARDEN / THE STRAND
12
35
50
51
CHELSEA / KENSINGTON / NOTTING HILL
53
47
54
11
4
32
15

NEWINGTON GREEN / DALSTON / HACKNEY

Scan to get
the map

SHOREDITCH / SPITALFIELDS

CLERKENWELL

SOUTHWARK

30 Bar Italia (p. 115)
31 Sager + Wilde (p. 119)
32 Aesop (p. 123)
33 Alex Eagle Studio (p. 127)
34 Coal Drops Yard (p. 131)
35 Dover Street Market (p. 133)
36 House of Hackney (p. 135)
37 Labour and Wait (p. 137)
38 magCulture (p. 139)
39 Margaret Howell (p. 141)
40 Perfumer H (p. 143)
41 Present & Correct (p. 147)
42 The Monocle Shop (p. 151)
43 Selfridges (p. 155)
44 The Barbican (p. 161)
45 Isokon Gallery (p. 165)
46 Kenwood House (p. 167)
47 Leighton House (p. 169)
48 Lisson Gallery (p. 173)
49 National Portrait Gallery (p. 177)
50 Sadie Coles HQ (p. 181)
51 Serpentine Gallery (p. 183)
52 Tate Modern (p. 187)
53 The Design Museum (p. 189)
54 Victoria and Albert Museum (p. 191)

Mads Arlien-Søborg is a Copenhagen-based journalist and lifestyle expert. He holds a master's degree in modern Culture and Communication from University of Copenhagen. Mads has worked with design, fashion and lifestyles for many years. He has hosted several television shows about travel, design and architecture.

New Mags is more than a bookstore; it's a destination where art and literature converge, offering a select array of lifestyle books, magazines, and accessories. Founded in 2016 in Horsens, Jutland by Jesper Svangård and Jesper Oxholm Mikkelsen. Their dream of a space that not only stores but celebrates books culminated in the opening of their first showroom in Copenhagen in 2021.

NOTES

NOTES

NOTES

Front cover:
© Mads Arlien-Søborg

Destination:
© Mads Arlien-Søborg

Neighbourhoods:
© Mads Arlien-Søborg / Georgi Kalaydzhiev / Richard Evans / James Moore / Jolene Bakery & Restaurant / Monocle Shop / Kuro Coffee / @kamil_lens

Stay:
Art'otel London Battersea Power Station: © Klunderbie
Bermond Locke: © Edmund Dabney
Inhabit Southwick Street: Courtesy of Inhabit Southwick Street
Lime Tree hotel: Courtesy of Lime Tree hotel
One Hundred Shoreditch: Courtesy of One Hundred Shoreditch
Shoreditch House: Courtesy of Shoreditch House
The Hoxton Southwark: Courtesy of The Hoxton
The Lost Poet: Courtesy of The Lost Poet
The Newman: Courtesy of The Newman Hotel

Taste:
Bar Italia: © Lenny Di Lorenzo / peacture.com
Brawn: © John Carey / Tom Cockram
Cadet: Courtesy of Cadet
Café Cecilia: © Maureen M Evans maureenme.com
Café Petiole: © Anton Rodriguez
Common Breads: © Felix Speller
Goodbye Horses: Sam Harris / Adam Kang
Greenberry Café: Courtesy of Greenberry Café
Jolene Bakery & Restaurant: Courtesy of Jolene Bakery & Restaurant
Kuro Coffee: Courtesy of Kuro Coffee
Leo's Bar & Restaurant: Courtesy of Leo's Bar & Restaurant
Morchella: © Stuart Mills
Noisy Oyster: Courtesy of Noisy Oyster
Oma: Courtesy of Oma
Perilla: Courtesy of Perilla
Rochelle Canteen: © Emma Louise Pudge
Sager + Wilde: Courtesy of Sager + Wilde
Sessions Arts Club: Courtesy of Sessions Arts Club
St. JOHN Bread and Wine: © Stefan Johnson
St. JOHN Smithfield: © Stefan Johnson
The River Café Café: © Matthew Donaldson
Toklas: © Kyle Caddey / Ola Smit / Courtesy of Sessions Toklas

Shop:
Aesop: Courtesy of Aesop
Alex Eagle Studio: Courtesy of Alex Eagle Studio
Coal Drop Yard: © Luke Hayes / Raquel Diniz / John Sturrock c/o King's Cross
Dover Street Market: Courtesy of Dover Street Market
House of Hackney: Courtesy of House of Hackney
Labour and Wait: Courtesy of Labour and Wait
magCulture: Courtesy of magCulture
Margaret Howell: © John Hooper
Perfumer H: © Lesley Lau @lesley_lau_
Present & Correct: Courtesy of Present & Correct
Monocle Shop: Courtesy of Monocle Shop
Selfridges: © Andrew-Meredith / Tim Charles / TDM.Space

Explore:
Barbican: Pexels
Isokon Gallery: © Tom De Gay, Isokon Gallery / Pritchard Papers, UEA
Kenwood House: © English Heritage
Leighton House: © Leighton House Museum, RBKC
Lisson Gallery: © Dexter Dalwood / Yu Hong / Ken Adlard / Courtesy of Lisson Gallery
National Portrait Gallery: © Olivier Hess / David Parry / Katie Morrison / Matthew Barney / Ugo Rondinone / Eva Herzog / Courtesy the Artist and Sadie Coles HQ, London
Serpentine Gallery: © Mass Studies, Iwan Baan / Courtesy of Serpentine Gallery
Tate Modern: Unsplash
The Design Museum: © Gravity Road / Hufton + Crow / Gareth Gardner
Victoria and Albert Museum / V&A East: © Peter Kelleher / Courtesy of Victoria and Albert Museum / Hufton + Crow / Alan Williams photography

NEW MAGS CITY GUIDE
LONDON

Editor-In-Chief: Mads Arlien-Søborg
Publisher: New Mags
Sales: Jesper Svangård, New Mags

Art Direction: Studio8585
Design Director: Mario Depicolzuane
Design & Layout: Benja Pavlin, Varshini KVSS

ISBN: 97887-85374-21-9

1st Edition 2026
Printed at Print Best, Estonia, 2026

Published in 2026 by New Mags
& Helmin Publishing

New Mags city guides are available at special discounts when purchased in quantity for premiums and promotions as well as fundraising or educational use. For details, contact post@new-mags.com or the address below.

Buy the Books Online: new-mags.com

New Mags, Office & Distribution
Vejlevej 13, 8700 Horsens, Denmark
new-mags.com

NEW MAGS

Helmin Publishing
Nivå Strandpark 21, 1, 2990 Nivå, Denmark
helminpublishing.dk

This book contains a curated selection of the editor's favourite places and should be used for its intended purpose, as a guide. It is by no means comprehensive of all the amazing locations the city has to offer. Since changes may have occurred since publication, we recommend using the contact information for each location to ensure up-to-date details.

The editor and publisher wish to express their gratitude to everyone who played a role in making this book possible: the staff, friends and families, brands, and organizations. A big thank you to Fujifilm® for giving us the opportunity to create beautiful city images for the book.